I0211564

Angus Cerini is a writer, performer and theatre-maker from Melbourne. In 2014 he won the Griffin Award for New Australian Playwriting for *The Bleeding Tree*. His work has been presented by companies including Sydney Theatre Company, Malthouse Theatre and Arena Theatre Company, and been awarded prizes including the Patrick White Playwrights' Award and the Victorian Premier's Literary Award. His self-produced work has toured locally and internationally.

Shari Sebbens, Airlie Dodds and Paula Arundell in Griffin Theatre Company's 2015 production. (Photo: Brett Boardman)

THE BLEEDING TREE

ANGUS CERINI

Currency Press, Sydney

CURRENCY PLAYS

First published in 2015
by Currency Press Pty Ltd,
PO Box 2287, Strawberry Hills, NSW, 2012, Australia
enquiries@currency.com.au
www.currency.com.au

in association with Griffin Theatre Company

This revised edition first published in 2017.

Copyright: *The Bleeding Tree* © Angus Cerini, 2015, 2017; Introduction © Diana Simmonds 2017

COPYING FOR EDUCATIONAL PURPOSES

The Australian *Copyright Act 1968* (Act) allows a maximum of one chapter or 10% of this book, whichever is the greater, to be copied by any educational institution for its educational purposes provided that that educational institution (or the body that administers it) has given a remuneration notice to Copyright Agency Limited (CAL) under the Act.

For details of the CAL licence for educational institutions contact CAL, 11/66 Goulburn St, Sydney, NSW, 2000; tel: within Australia 1800 066 844 toll free; outside Australia 61 2 9394 7600; fax: 61 2 9394 7601; email: info@ copyright.com.au

COPYING FOR OTHER PURPOSES

Except as permitted under the Act, for example a fair dealing for the purposes of study, research, criticism or review, no part of this book may be reproduced, stored in a retrieval system, or transmitted in any form or by any means without prior written permission. All enquiries should be made to the publisher at the address above.

Any performance or public reading of *The Bleeding Tree* is forbidden unless a licence has been received from the author or the author's agent. The purchase of this book in no way gives the purchaser the right to perform the play in public, whether by means of a staged production or a reading. All applications for public performance should be addressed c/- Currency Press.

Cataloguing-in-publication data for this title is available from the National Library of Australia website: www.nla.gov.au

Cover design by Studio Emma for Currency Press.
Typeset by Dean Nottle for Currency Press.

Currency Press acknowledges the Traditional Owners of the Country on which we live and work. We pay our respects to all Aboriginal and Torres Strait Islander Elders, past and present.

Contents

Paula Arundell in Griffin Theatre Company's 2015 production. (Photo: Brett Boardman)

INTRODUCTION

Diana Simmonds

Population, Pictures and Poetry

Performed by just three actors, *The Bleeding Tree* is populated by many other characters. They are the inhabitants of the small rural town on whose outskirts the action takes place. Also present is the corpse of whom the lead actor says: 'Girls, I think your father is dead.' The trio is unnamed but it is immediately clear that one is the mother, the other two her young adult daughters.

It's no surprise and no spoiler that the man is dead, murdered, brutally. The play's opening line is a haiku to that effect: 'With a bullet hole through your neck, numbskull of yours never looked so fine.' It's also a line that sets the tone for all that follows: laconic, poetic, rich and raw.

The use of the word 'numbskull' in this context is another pointer to the play and all that transpires. A more correct – prosaic – sentence would have given what we are hearing as something like, 'that head of yours has never looked so fine,' (after being bashed in by his distraught offspring) but would be neither so vivid nor so expansive. Because the common meaning of the word 'numbskull' is 'a stupid or foolish person' – we are also being told this as well as being given further subtle colouration through the discrete ideas of 'numb' and 'skull'.

Although 'numbskull' is not Cockney rhyming slang (the unique semi-dialect that accompanied convicts from London to Port Jackson) it lays the groundwork for what we hear from time to time throughout the play. For instance, when a neighbour enters the house and almost trips over the dead man their response is: 'Shit he see it, the old man's peg.'

To a Cockney, pegs aren't as straightforward as mere laundry props. Rhyming slang dictates someone can be 'light on their pins' (a good dancer) or that 'me pegs are barkin',' (my legs are aching). Thus, if legs are 'pin pegs' (clothes pegs once carved from single scraps of wood and sold door to door) then they are also 'pins' and 'pegs', as nothing can be better than a shortened version of anything. So, when the neighbour is close to the body of the murdered man, what's visible from beneath the blanket covering him is his leg. (There is also a peg leg of course, but that's another story.)

This vivacious use of language is characteristic of Cerini's work and in *The Bleeding Tree* he uses it to create extraordinarily tangible images of people and places that exist only in the imaginations of the audience: there are never more than the three actors on stage and precious few props. The pictures are all in the mind.

Angus Cerini is a playwright and performer whose body of written work could be encapsulated in something he said at the National Play Festival in 2013, where his play *Scowl* was performed. During an interview at the festival with Tom Healey, he observed, 'White men run the world so if the world is crap, well it's white men we have to look at.' Go back over his creative life and it's plain he has been doing just that throughout.

Cerini's early artistic work was mainly exploratory when approaching themes of violence (*Saving Henry*, 2003). Then he began to dip below the surface of hopelessness and its resulting psychosis (*Wretch*, 2007) but still did not go further – no redemption, no solutions. Abuse – by individuals and/or society – underpinned *Save For Crying* (2011) in which the intellectually disabled Luv and Alfie suffer not only their calamitous lives but also are tormented by Ratspunk, a lowlife who's nevertheless a step higher up the food-scraps chain than they. And then in 2014 he wrote *The Bleeding Tree*.

Revenge, Rage and Redemption

In both *Wretch* and *Detest* there is a character who, while not the same in either, performs a role that prefigures the monstrous triumph of *The Bleeding Tree*. In the earlier plays the killer and rapist of an elderly woman is himself beaten to death by a young man. But there is no mercy or absolution, conventional or otherwise, for what could be seen as at least an anti-hero. For differing reasons his fate is sealed and it has nothing to do with the still perceptible influence in Western popular culture of the US *Comic Book Code*, 1954 which insisted that, 'good shall triumph over evil'. Yet in these more complex and – one can hope

– more thoughtful times, what is 'good' and what is 'evil'?

According to White Ribbon (Australia's campaign to prevent men's violence against women), one in three women have experienced violence perpetrated by a person known to them. One in five women over the age of 18 have been stalked. Over 12 months, on average, one woman is killed every week by a current or former partner. Domestic and family violence is the principal cause of homelessness for women and children. Indigenous women and girls are 35 times more likely than the wider female population to be hospitalised due to family violence. In Australia, one in four children are exposed to domestic violence.

These bland numbers and the neutrality of the language ('person', 'stalk', 'partner', 'domestic') make relatively benign a national disgrace: a third of women experience violence, and 20% of women can expect to be stalked. Women's activist group Destroy the Joint tallies the violent deaths of Australian women: the figure for 2016 was 71. Already, by the end of January 2017, five more have been murdered. We can expect a quarter of our children to be exposed to domestic violence. And overwhelmingly there is one basic cause, whether the victims are black or white or any colour in between; let's go back to Cerini in 2013: 'White men run the world so if the world is crap, well it's white men we have to look at.'

The Bleeding Tree does look at it and with the playwright's characteristically unflinching and unsentimental eyes. Yet this time he goes beyond merely looking, merely recording. He takes the plunge into a place that is still problematic – what if? What if the characters no longer simply experience and reflect those experiences but do something – actively – about them? He sets out a story that illustrates traditional concepts and characters of good and evil and one way or another, he inverts them. Like it or not: he gives a solution to this particular question.

His setting is a timeless, impoverished farm where a family ekes out an existence. The lives of the three females are punctuated by the seasons, their chores and the intermittent drunken violence of the husband/father. Out the back of their tumbledown house is the bleeding tree – a massive one with a suitable branch from which a carcass can be slung and slaughtered. It's only logical that this is where the man's body should be hung after he has lashed out one too many times and been bludgeoned and shot to death by his no-longer long-suffering wife and daughters.

It's only logical because we know by sly, slight means what his absence and presence mean to his family: when a neighbour arrives to investigate a gunshot being heard in the neighbourhood he asks, 'Everything alright is it?' And the answer is, 'Well he ain't home yet, so yeah, so far it's fine.' It is at once sardonic and the essence of their lives. The contrast and transposition of the norms are also found in scenes where roughly rhyming lines – doggerel-like and laced with dark comedy – are employed to paint an otherwise ghastly picture:

- Action stations ladies, heave how she goes.
- Heave lift drag what a blow.
- Heavy as buggery this old prick.
- And count of three together now girls, that's the trick.
- And drag and lift, drop.
- Breath, catch it, count to three go.
- And heave.
- And drag and lift, go.
- Over the stoop, down the step.
- And drag lift, go.
- Out behind the shed, feet in the rope, three of us lifting, tie off the dead bloke.
- On the block and tight he holds.
- Heave together now girls and up she goes.
- Lookit ya now ya old soak.
- And lift.
- Blood rushes down from his legs.
- All together on my count of three and lift.
- Arms flop down past his head.
- Three, and lift.
- Not going nowhere in a real hurry anytime soon eh old prick.
- Lumps hanging useless bang against his cold head.
- Geez Mum, why'd you get with this prick?
- Dangling there in the sky.

- Blood gone drained out that hole in his neck.
- King of the castle is ya?
- Scary now is ya?
- Ha!

In *The Bleeding Tree* the tables are turned – this is no secret – but what is in doubt is what will become of the patricidal girls and the mariticidal wife. Convention and the middle class would demand retribution. An eye for an eye and a tooth for a tooth may have been a rollicking Old Testament tenet – but not for women. In popular culture in particular, women and the lower classes could not be allowed to 'get away with it'. This is thanks partly to such rulebooks as the aforementioned Comic Book Code as well as the Motion Picture Production Code (or Hays Code). Although both were American, their effects permeated Australia and anyway were in tune with the mores of the seemingly never-ending Menzies era. Before the rise (and mid-century hegemony) of screen culture, there were still (unwritten) rule books to shore up white, male, middle-class society. Crime could not be allowed to pay, and neither could the wishes and wellbeing of women be prioritised. For instance, popular opera of the 19th century was home to transgressive heroines such as Mimi in *La Bohème* and Violetta in *La Traviata*, who had to die in order to preserve male domination of polite society; tuberculosis was a diversion.

The status quo in the unnamed small town of *The Bleeding Tree* is not as immutable as nineteenth- or twentieth-century America or Europe however, and what occurs is hair-raising and unpredictable. It's a blend of Gothic horror, morality tale and revenge tragedy writ small which is also – as befits a drama of life and death 'Down Under' – drolly upside down in its outcome. The final desperate rage of the killers gives way to that most satisfying but politically incorrect of actions: blood-drenched, successful revenge. Like the first blow itself, it's a thrilling concept and has an indelible place in drama – whether on stage or in life. And then the unthinkable happens. Instead of the perpetrators getting their just desserts, as prescribed, the various visitors to the house gradually make it clear that the town is not in the mood for biblical retribution. Instead, they offer possibilities, reasons, excuses and ideas to explain the man's sudden disappearance; they want to help!

Will the women be able to live with their sin? Are they 'forgiven' by others? It's a profound dilemma and, like the killing itself, not one that could be resolved by any of us – with any reliability – before the fact. No matter the subject matter there is one thing that unites all in Angus Cerini's work and it is that he does not offer flip solutions, easy answers or fridge-magnet homilies. Instead, he simultaneously holds up a mirror and a magnifying glass: what we see in them is up to us. In *The Bleeding Tree* it could be something akin to, 'There but for the grace of God go I.'

Diana Simmonds is a Sydney-based theatre reviewer.

ACKNOWLEDGEMENTS

The Bleeding Tree was developed with the support of Playwriting Australia and the Department of Performance Studies at the University of Sydney as part of the National Script Workshops 2014. It was further developed with the support of the Victorian Government through Creative Victoria in 2015. Immense thanks to Amanda Macri, Alice Poujois-Enari and Playwriting Australia, Dr Laura Ginters (and students) at the University of Sydney and all of the artists involved with the developments: Jeanette Cronin, Susie Dee, Lucy Goleby, Aimee Horne, Jenni Medway, Tim Roseman, Kate Sherman, Iain Sinclair, Sarah Snook and Nicci Wilks. And to the entire creative team of the first production led by Lee Lewis, to all at Griffin, the Griffin Award and the sponsors that make this production possible—an especially enormous thank you.

playwriting
australia

CREATIVE
VICTORIA

State
Government
Victoria

A NOTE FROM THE AUTHOR

It was enormously enjoyable writing *The Bleeding Tree*. To revel in the downfall of someone who preys on others and to envisage a community joining in on that destruction.

The first few words for this play came out very quickly, and simply as a few jotted pages responding to a call from my friend Susie Dee—who was working with Kate Sherman and Nicci Wilks on a creative development in Albury Wodonga at the time—exploring the idea of 'the scars women carry'.

I had no idea those few pages would bug me sufficiently to become a full and actual play. I had no way of knowing that Playwriting Australia, Sydney University and Creative Victoria would all provide assistance in its development, or that this little play about women fighting back would win the Griffin Prize and that Lee Lewis would jump on board and guide it with such care and sensitivity to the stage. And in so doing introduce me to the charms and powers of that tiny but mighty powerhouse that is Griffin Theatre Company. And to that Griffin team of Renee, Verity, Steve, Edwina, Paula, Shari and Airlie making my heart almost burst with pride with each performance. And even less an idea that our production would have a return season at the Sydney Theatre Company. I mean they say from little things big things grow, but this is surely taking that to extremes!

Perhaps the enjoyment I've had writing *The Bleeding Tree* comes back to the fact that lots of small but powerful moments and individuals have combined to bring this play to life. And perhaps societal changes are likewise brought about the same way. And if we can do it with a piece of theatre, then there's really no excuse why we can't do it to eradicate crimes of violence against the vulnerable.

I hope you enjoy this experience of *The Bleeding Tree*.

A note on the script

In choosing to present this script without lines allocated to particular characters I am hoping the reader will engage with the work more as a poem, or a stream of consciousness. While a version of the script exists with character names allocated (and is used in production), I tend to think such practicalities get in the way of the thrust of the piece. Least of all by giving these characters names.

AC, 2017

The Bleeding Tree was first produced by Griffin Theatre Company at the SBW Stables Theatre, Sydney, on 31 July 2015, with the following cast:

Paula Arundell
Airlie Dodds
Shari Sebbens

Director, Lee Lewis
Designer, Renée Mulder
Lighting Designer, Verity Hampson
Composer, Steve Toulmin

CHARACTERS

Three women play a mother and her two daughters.

SETTING

The action occurs in a farmhouse some distance from a rural town.

I

– With a bullet hole through your neck, that numbskull of yours never looked so fine.
– Rest in peace Daddy numbskull.
– Ta ta Daddy ya sick bundle of shit.
– Bye bye Daddy you misery heap of shit.

– Lookit him there all on the floor.
– Still.
– Prick's not moving no more.
– How's them tricks you played now so sick and strange old man?
– Rest in peace how's that treating ya?
– Your stuffed-up river of broken skin and knitting bones.
– And with dead eyes staring back from the floor.
– Dead eyes and you inside them never coming back no more.
– Rest in peace Daddy numbskull.
– Eat sick in hell.

– Mum wipes her cheek absent like, looks at her flowers spilt on the floor.
– Mum.
– Looks up absent like.
– Mum?
– Yes girls.
– Where's Dad gone Mum?
– Gone the way that bird went gone girls.
– That dead one never come back that one?
– That's the one.
– Off back beyond the never-never is he Mum?

– Out back beyond the black stump is he Mum?
– Gone looking for trouble somewhere is he Mum?
– Couldn't tell ya girls, can only tell you what I know.
– What you know then Mum?
– Yeah what you know?
– Black panther seen sometimes in the hills, never prove it.
– Lurking in a lake maybe, like that?
– Yeah like that one maybe, like that one.

– The stink of him lies flat like a tack.
– Dead hands lying flat by your side, not much use now are they arse-hat?
– Loving like yours old man like a canker in the throat.
– Absently holds her chin.
– Holds a hand against the bit of blood.
– Holds her face firm, looks down at him.
– Where's he gone you say Mum?
– Couldn't tell you girls.

– Quiet.
– Creaking of the old dump he wouldn't do a scrap of fixing.
– His mud boots, coat and hat by the door.
– Petals caught in her hair.
– He's not getting up.
– Don't think so love.
– Shouldn't have tried it eh Mum?
– Don't think that neither love.

– Same old story, heard it a thousand times before, too many times to mention.
– Same old story, know it good, this time pushed too far.

- The screen door bangs, standing there, hulking like something you know to fear.
- Dinner, where's his dinner the man?
- Out the back ya sap of a man.
- Don't say it can hear inside your head.
- Knows anything he decides to know.
- You say what you say what you say?
- Said ya dinner's out back ya half-baked shred of a man.
- Bright stinking face sways what you say?
- Said ya dinner's out back where the pigs slop feed.
- Too much lip I take that face and wipe it off you got that?
- Yeah and we had a picnic we did Dad.
- Picnic without ya curse on a house.
- Picnic without your dad?
- Picnic out back cos it's her birthday.
- Birthday? Whose birthday?
- Looks dumbfounded.
- Stupid lump of shit.
- Not nobody birthday, a trap for you ya ugly stupid prick.
- Birthday is it eh girl day of the sun? Like when you was just a glimmer in me eye.
- Took her didn't say yes, just claimed her isn't that right ya son of a gun?
- Like a man pretending he's not a dog.
- Woman speak.
- Instructs again.
- Woman man say speak.
- Snarls again.
- Going the way of the dodo if can we help it.
- That's for sure.
- Try to smile at his sick head.

- The sight of it makes us all sick.
- We got cake out there for you too old prick.
- All made out with your name written in stink.
- Picnic old dad, out back.
- Picnic out back where the animals feed.
- Place for you in amongst their shit.
- Fit right in you useless drunk prick.
- Got the apeshit on him now, mottled angry and red.
- Would youse take a look at that.
- Ya don't scare us.
- Useless no-hoper you poor excuse for a dad.
- Lookit him you lot, what a useless fuck-head.
- Roars with rage.
- Come here ya whore.
- Whack, dodge the drunk prick.
- Nice one old loser, got any more?
- And bang just like that I gets him, buckles to his knees.
- Just like that like that to his knees.
- Buckle him down, whack with me trick.
- The old broom handles tied together like one solid thick stick.
- Spins with surprise looks at his legs.
- Collapsing beneath him, nice bloody trick!
- Losing the strength to hold him, his pegs they do fail, and she moves up close to conk him on the head.
- Whack!
- Down she blows.
- Whack to his legs.
- Easy he falls like lead.
- And whack to his head.
- Hate you we do.
- Hate you.

– And he's not sure what's happening.
– Drunk mind is racing.
– But like birthday girl with all her wishes come true she rises up, gun in her hand.
– He's flat on his face twelve-gauge on his neck.
– And slow so slow he turns.
– Turns right over.
– Stares right up.
– Standing there above him the three Lady Luck.
– And he sees our faces, hatred at him yuk.
– And he sees our sweet faces turned loathing and muck.
– And he sees the three ladies, woman and her girls.
– And the fear in his eyes spreads like piss on his legs.
– But no chance for pleading cos with that she pulls down and blows.
– And just like that.
– He's got no neck.
– And with that he's lying there dead.
– Shotgun still pressed against his neck.
– And with that he's stopped doing anything more.
– Thank Christ the prick is dead.
– Thank Christ the prick is dead.
– Girls, I think your father's dead.
– I knocked his knees out.
– I conked his head.
– I shot that house-clown in the neck.

– Silence.
– Whoa.
– Did him Mum.
– Lookit him spread.
– Geez, he's really really dead.

– Yep.

– Quiet.
– The three of us.
– Fuck.
– Fuck.
– He's dead right?
– He's dead.
– Quiet.
– Exhale.
– Deep breath.
– Dead.

– Now what?
– We get him outside is what. We wipe up his whatnot. Cover him with a blanket. Sight of him makes me sick.
– Blink.
– Blink.
– He's dead.
– Well don't just stand there, go.
– Get to work the three of us.
– Shakes still taking us, every little bit sometimes comes up choking us.
– Dead.
– Dead.
– Enough girls, get the job done.

– Wall looking clean?
– Like brand bloody new.
– Floor too.
– Soaked in places, onto that too.
– Good girls.

– Now what?

– Get him outside. Take a leg and an arm and an arm and a leg.

– Onto the blanket, roll him on, roll him on.

– Okay on the count of three.

– And one, two…

– He's heavy.

– Christ.

– Okay again.

– Three, two…

– Bloody hell.

– Okay work together, and breathe in together, on my count of three.

– One, two, three.

– And heave, stumped he's big.

– Stupid lumpen lard of dead stupid sick.

II

– Knock crack tappity snap.

– Holy hell what's that?

– Knock at the door that's what's that.

– Knock at the door.

– Knock at the door.

– Knock.

– Crap.

– Shit.

– Who's knocking?

– Shit.

– Quick.

– Who's knocking at the door?

– Fuck.

– Crap.

– Shit.

– Quick get him behind the thing.

– Drag him quick, wash up after him.

– Knock. Loud. Insistent. Like a fly trying to get in.

– Or a dog.

– Knock.

– Or a whining cat.

– Okay okay hold your horses.

– Blanket over him.

– She's cool as anything.

– Blanket over him.

– Cool it girls, nothing wrong. Sit.

– No.

– I said sit.

– Mum no. Too suss waiting like.

– Just over there you sit.

– Wake us all up.

– Knock is what, wake us all up.

– Tired. Looking tired. Playing tired.

– Knock. Insistent it is.

– I said I'm coming!

– Just tired, just been woken, bloody knocking.

– Who's it coming?

– Creak, sneak, it's Mister Jones.

– Mister Jones?

– Jones, the nice one.

– Not his son?

– His old man one, nice one.

– If he comes in, if he comes in.

– He won't come in. Throw the blanket over him.
– He won't come in.
– He knows and he's here, why's he here?
– He's not coming in, not know a thing.
– I look alright girls I look okay?
– Creak.
– Breathe.
– Open the thing.

– Hello Mister Jones.
– Hello says he.
– Your old man get in okay says he?
– I ain't seen him yet. You got him in the truck?
– He was swaying off this way, and I hear a shot. Everything all right
   is it?
– I don't hear a shot.
– Figure something's maybe not right.
– Haven't seen him, been on the drink. That's what I think.
– That's for sure.

– Everything alright is it? Jones takes a sniff.
– Well he ain't home yet, so yeah, so far it's fine.
– Maybe out on the paddocks old smithy took him for a fox.
– Maybe he got it in the guts.
– Useless prick.
– Well he's not the brightest spark your bloke—pretty bloody useless
   the drunk silly prick.
– Crimson he goes does Jones.
– Sorry Missus, rude thing to say.
– Jones and the shame on him, swearing in front of the ladies.
– Ha, ladies.

- Not you that's for sure.
- Shut your face you.
- Girls! Woke us up with your knocking man gave us a fright.
- Haven't seen him then, not come in the door?
- Nah, no sign at all.
- Mum's cool as she is.
- Never could tell she just put a hole in the bastard's neck.
- I dropped him at the knees.
- I conked him on the head.
- No sign of him at all.

- Spies her face where the red welt is swelling.
- Instinctively touches his own chin, rubs it, throws his eyes down...
- Not sure where to look, what to say, whether to go away.
- Rubs his face, his hands, his head.
- Mumbling, stumbling, casting around, thinking what Mister Jones?
- Heard a gunshot one is all. Shouldn't I come through, just to check the all clear?
- Nobody here to stress about a thing, us three got it eh girls?
- Not here Mister is what we is saying.
- Well I should come in, say I been here and I can go away and I can say I ain't seen nothing. They'd kill me something happen and old Jones do nothing.
- Stamps his feet, calls out a bit, Pete.
- Pete ain't here Mister, ain't seen him yet.
- He steps on in nothing Mum can do.
- Have to let him pass, the done thing to do.
- Look.
- Mum.
- Shit.
- Look the bloody thing.

- Clear as bloody day.
- One leg, sticking out.
- Just the bloody one.
- Edge of his trouser and his boot.
- Clear as the day.
- Blanket stopped short.
- Swallow down the sick.
- Shit he see it, the old man's peg?
- Shuffle stand in front of it.

- Eyes come settle on her face, fix on the red blast coming up angry and swollen.
- Hand reaches out gentle like.
- Eyes drop, pushing it back down, whatever it is that comes up inside of him.
- Sorrow that is.
- He got sorrow is what that is.
- Looking down chewing on his sorrow.
- Back up again at her head.
- Taking in her face beaten red.
- Tears maybe, glisten in his eyes.
- You bump your head?
- A something inside Mister Jones he don't understand.
- Reaches out, a single rose petal caught in her hair.
- So gentle like.
- Holds it between two big fat fingers.
- Looks at it, kinda soft and strange like.
- Rubs it in between those two clumsy pads.
- Flower in your hair, welt on your chin?
- Was just trying to get the old girl in her stall, nothing serious, just small.

- Bloody animal, bloody animal.
- Jones growls, eyes flare.
- Yeah, kick and scream, bumped me hard he did.
- Bloody bloody shaking his head.
- Animal bloody animal under his breath.
- Something cold on that kids.
- Something cold on that kids.
- Giving us directions.
- Bloody stupid man with his stupid man directions.
- You help your mum out girls.
- Glare at him, old Mister Jones.
- Yeah, course Mister Jones.
- Yeah course Mister Jones.
- Man reckons he knows.
- Stupid old idiot Mister Jones.
- Quiet like—if you need anything?
- Just a thing Jones, be better in no time.
- Bloody animal deserves to be put down. I find him take the drunken dog down.
- Was the mare Jones, not a mutt.
- Only thing for it sometimes, if he goes bad gotta put the thing down.
- Cut your losses feed him to the ground.
- Take off the dead wood make the others strong.

- Walks slow to the wall, towards the divan and him there, straight for the dead leg.
- Stands bloody hell right next to it.
- Bloody right next to it.
- Holy hell does he see?
- Holy hell no please don't see.

– Silence like a curtain being drawn he stares out past the dead lawn.
– Out at the moon and the paddocks bare.
– Just standing looking for the answers might find out there.
– Sees the fields and the moon dripping with bloody.
– And he sees those smartarse stars and the pouty clouds.
– And the wind banging on the tin shed roof.
– And chews on his own face and he don't say a thing.
– Quiet.
– Quiet.
– He's staring out there but right into our souls.

– And he kicks it.
– Shit.
– He just kicked it.
– Looks back around face gone changed.
– A snarl and a sneer clear as the day.
– He just kicked it.
– He did yeah?
– Yep, he kicked it.
– Kicked it yeah?
– Yeah he totally kicked it totally kicked it yeah.
– He knows it the old man's lying there.

– Speaks his throat opens, clears.
– Go on then.
– Yeah…
– Drawls the thing.
– Yeah see I reckon…
– Get the thing out of him someone bloody help him.
– Yeah see I reckon…

– Spit it out man.

– Yeah see I reckon maybe old mate's gone got himself confused by the night. Was pretty pissed when I left him out at the drive. Yeah heard a shot out there, yep heard that alright. And you says you hasn't seen him, isn't that right?

– Nod.

– Nod.

– Nod.

– Well he sure ain't here.

– Kicks it.

– Nah no sign of him here.

– And another one to be sure.

– Kicks him.

– Holy hell, lays the boot right in.

– But not letting on he's not just got a story to tell.

– And I dropped him off down the end of your road, and you hasn't seen him since he left for the pub. But I hear that shot going off, close it was too. Man in his state. Got a tad worried. Just wanted to check up he got in all right. Lots of hunters out of late.

– Kicks him.

– Maybe best he's out there sleeping it off. Pretty famous for his pissed fists your old bloke. Maybe he gone walk off visit someone he ever do that?

– Death eyes say wants to stamp on him is what.

– Says you hasn't seen him, and sure as hell he ain't here. And it's gonna be hot tomorrow.

– Hot tomorrow, like every day.

– Yeah, hot tomorrow, if he's knocked his head and fallen down, only last a day or two with that sun beating down.

– Yeah if he's knocked his head won't last long in this hot.

– Three days lying out there in the sun. I wouldn't like his chances. Sorry love.

– I hope he's alright.

– Is he going to be okay?

– We bung on the lies make us all a happy song.

– They say you know this time of year, three days hanging up a tree the most you get before there's not much left to see. Them flies start their work, then the creatures they tell come speak for the rest. Yeah, three days hanging from a tree. Cleans up the bones, a real sight to see. Or not—if you know what I mean.

– Hanging from a tree?

– Something to consider anyway—if he was out there—fallen down that is, and somehow hanging from a tree. Hanging like from your one out back there you got for the cow bleeding and the carcass prep. A tree like that a real spot on spot.

– Eyes twinkling above a filthy grin.

– But you hasn't seen him so that's kind of beside the point. Like but if he was strung up from that bleeding tree is all I'm saying is what.

Or maybe gone visit a relative is he? Maybe got some sister or some such is he? Sure I heard mention of that at the pub. Yeah he got some sister or some such he gone to see?

– Sister?

– Tree?

– Maybe he mention he got a family member go see?

– He may that he may be.

– Fallen down maybe out there, less he's off visiting someone.

– Visiting someone, yeah I see.

– Said once he had a sister or some such maybe so and so…?

– Sister?

– He got a sister maybe, I got me stories all confused maybe?

– No, he has a sister.

– Yeah, that's what I heard.

– Three days you say?

– Yeah, well I been and there's no sign of him that's for sure.

– Sorry to bother you ladies it being so late and all.

- Takes in that welt on the chin.
- That bloody horse. Better off dead. You girls need anything, before I'm off to bed?
- No thanks Mister Jones.
- All good thanks Mister Jones.
- Well I hope he makes it home safe, him and his bones.

- And relief.
- Relief.
- Night Mister Jones.

- But creak creak, he's standing there again.
- Shit was all that just a joke?
- Standing there again, holding the hat and the coat.
- Bloody hell the coat and the hat.
- That fella of yours, stupid on the drink, left his bloody coat and hat in me truck he did. Was wearing 'em at the pub he was, we all can say.
- He did?
- He did?
- Best put 'em in me truck eh, lest I see him on the way.
- Quiet, stare held.
- So if he turns up tell him I've got 'em.
- And he goes silent with all he knows.
- And if anyone asks, I'll say at the pub no sign of nothing.
- And he grins like a champion that old Mister Jones.
- That bloody champion old Mister Jones.

III

- Action stations ladies, heave how she goes.
- Heave lift drag what a blow.

– Heavy as buggery this old prick.
– And count of three together now girls, that's the trick.
– And drag and lift, drop.
– Breath, catch it, count to three go.
– And heave.
– And drag and lift, go.
– Over the stoop, down the step.
– And drag lift, go.
– Out behind the shed, feet in the rope, three of us lifting, tie off the dead bloke.
– On the block and tight he holds.
– Heave together now girls and up she goes.
– Lookit ya now ya old soak.
– And lift.
– Blood rushes down from his legs.
– All together on my count of three and lift.
– Arms flop down past his head.
– Three, and lift.
– Not going nowhere in a real hurry anytime soon eh old prick.
– Lumps hanging useless bang against his cold head.
– Geez Mum, why'd you get with this prick?
– Dangling there in the sky.
– Blood gone drained out that hole in his neck.
– King of the castle is ya?
– Scary now is ya?
– Ha!

– Neck juice spilling, dripping down into the dirt.
– Hands flopping useless clasping dead air.
– Lookit his eyes Mum!
– Lookit his hair.

– Lookit his beauty girls, such a sight to see. Tie the thing off, wrap it round the tree.

– High up all mighty now king of nothing you see.

– Swipe 'em away, flies in the night already itching.

– Blood gone dark with shadows curling.

– Meat call made out there in the dark. Hear that?

– The dogs out there scoping for a feed.

– Hurry on up with your padded feet brave.

– Bullet neck never looked so fine the way it does tonight.

– Shit we really killed him.

– Yep.

– Shit we really really killed him.

– White skin sick.

– Shit. Feel sick.

– Grins wearing thin.

– I feel not sure now.

– Cold tired sore now.

– We all feel the same. Come inside, enough for a night. Let's get this finished with. Buckets, soap.

– Up in them branches.

– Foxes smell it. Crows too.

– Shadow wings lift him right away.

– Piece by piece Mum?

– Dingoes have a go?

– Three days we'll know.

– Three days we'll know.

– Just three days to end him forever, three days to go.

IV

- The night settles on in with the smell of some sorta sweet rousing drifting by.
- Drinks passed round, walls wiped clean.
- Now girls, again, what you asking?
- Where's the dad gone Mum?
- Gone to see his sister love.
- Where's the old man gone Mum?
- Gone to see his sister.
- He don't have a sister Mum.
- You say that or not?
- He got a sister has got one for sure.
- Where's his sister Mum?
- We never got along.
- What's her name, this sister?
- A woman with a cruel stare like him—suit each other like crumbs in a tin.
- What's her name when they ask of this sister?
- Marj her name is. Yeah Marj is her name.
- Town that she from?
- Out there some place I couldn't name you.
- Had a run-in did it old Mum what you saying?
- Too right mate, too right.
- Tell us the tale of this sister they're after.
- When they ask where's he gone this bloke our father?
- Hallowed be thy name, thy kingdom come, on your sick earth no more your will be done.
- Dead now that old prick.
- Girls, no! You say that out loud you make a mistake.

- Went to the pub, never come back.
- Didn't see him after he gone to the pub.
- Off to work he went, says he was going to his sister's.
- What's her name?
- He's gone to his sister's, her name's Marjory Bastard. She lives up in the sun, what gone made her mad as her brother.
- What's her name?
- I told ya it's Marjory and she lives up north, where it's hot as all buggery, flies your best friends… like your shadow they is.
- Oh yeah?
- Believe it does ya?
- Not sure not sure.
- She had evil eyes—shoulda known it from the start.
- Just like her bloody brother.
- If only ya knew.
- The mother died, and this crone sees every other woman like a pretender for the throne. It's time to move away from here I says to him.
- Can't have her in our life no more.
- We stay here I'm embalmed.
- The going away was like a pleasure unimagined.
- Was like some strange idea come good—like a holiday card pinned to me heart.
- After six weeks of married hell we was on the road. Dusty, poor as a sack, clothes like card on me back. Belly full of nothing but air and dreams. And how bloody lovely. Land here to this hole in the earth. The minute you was born it got to starting.
- Throw the thing at the wall.
- Shut the thing up whore.
- Come in all hours waving his man stick around, beating his sicko song.
- Here ya go, wrap your lips round this, suck me a tune.

– Cunting it up against the all everything, oh here he is, Master Bloody Laughter.
– Sound of his truck, his tyres, his piss-poor way to be a man.
– A man like the best man ever if all you got to go on is a turd.
– Here's a shit on the side of the road, laid by a dog, now stand up next to it old man, there ya are, no bloody difference.
– You and that turd very bloody same thing.
– You both stink.
– You both a waste of time.
– Ya both hang around on everyone's shoe.
– Stinking out the place.
– Excreta of a man that's you.
– You old man you're like one of them ones you stand in, squelchy old man.
– Shitstink man.
– Shitstink man what come up between your toes. Use a stick poke it out. Rub your feet on grass but that stink gone stunk up every little bit of your smelling. Nothing but the stink of shit.
– That's him alright.
– Wipe him off, along with the snot and blood.
– Your woman place stings from his rage.
– Watch him snore and the fire logs fall, out of the grill and onto his face. Burning he is in your dreams so bright, excuses already lined up thick and fast.
– I come in and he's just all burnt up.
– Asleep in my bed and smoke gets me head.
– Stumble in and there he is.
– Ideas of death come regular as the day.
– Was his sister what started it.
– Too right it is aye.
– What's her name Mum, this bloody sister the one he gone to see?
– Her name is Marjory. Marjory Bloody Bastard.

– Before my time.
– Before we was born.
– And he is gone there, and not here and good riddance.
– Good riddance is what.

– Tired from all this.
– Tired and sick gone right through, enough of this.
– Breathe.
– Exhale.
– Tomorrow, a new day…

V

– That stink you stink never made such a sweet smell as this one come
   wafting from your dead heart. Flimsy show-body up there in the sky.
   All or nothing up against the wall so often had me. With time on our
   side this place was green. Had character, hope, future-making here
   with the fences all strong like rope. Never believe in dreams come
   true before.

– You reckon he knows anything in his head gone shot through?
– Dead he is, nup.
– Reckon though he gets it?
– Gets nothing, is dead.
– Nothing he gets?
– Nothing he gets.
– Reckon though he know what he done?
– How he hurt ya?
– How he gone done all that?

– Is it wrong of me glad he's gone?

– Glad is truthful what you're feeling.

– Glad he's dead now.

– Nothing wrong with glad.

– Dead gullet open to the moon. Awful shrinking face still trying to gasp out some words. What you got left to say you ain't said already? What's that? Can't hear you old man.

– Is we bad though, did we do wrong?

– You is joking what he done all that is you serious?

– Just wondering is we going to hell?

– If we's hell-going then what was we living before?

– White eyes hollow and move. Saying something to me is ya? Back from the grave to sneer some more? Say what old man, you say what I can't hear ya? Spit it out old man. Spit it out.

– You thinking about, what you thinking?

– First time he come in here showed me the things. Just thinking on that, how he loved us maybe?

– Love isn't that.

– Nah?

– Nah.

– Love's what then?

– Love's saving yourself from what you get given, turning it into choices you making.

– Selfish to think of that first.

– If you getting your beating and the showing things, what beauty in that you find yourself ugly?

– Ugly.

– Ugly he brings.

- Brings ugly when life is better.
- Ugly he comes stomping through with.
- You draw something, or build something.
- Rip it up, stamp on it; beauty makes itself just by being itself.
- Standing on beauty, never destroy it, still drawn it.
- Just underneath waiting to come back up again.
- Just waiting to come back up again.
- Just waiting for a fresh moment in time is what.
- Is what I'm thinking.

- Rolling eyes caught in the shapes of a wake. Pictures this you make? Licking your lips, I can't hear ya. Gaping hole flicking face still alive … What's this, two glinting eyes? In your neck? Holy hell is that a rat in your neck? Dear heaven and mercy, shadow of the sun, you got a rat in there chewing on your tongue. A bloody rat. Inside your head.

- She's talking at him look.
- Gone mad as can be?
- Nah I reckon having just a well-earned dreaming reverie.
- Big bloody word that is you.
- Yeah I is smart is why.

- And another. And some more. Moving shapes on the ground and all around. Flashes in the night through the dirt and up the trunk, down the rope to his oozing guts. Say all ashes to ashes and dust to dust, but holy hell never mentioned no rats but. Oh that's a delicious bloody prize for the beatings and the show. Eaten from the insides out a marvellous bloody show.

 Having a yummy old time feasting away in there is it Mr Rat?

 Howdy missus, how's your new life now?

 Feels a bit strange to be honest. You?

Yeah all good out here in his yummy bloody head.

Full as a goog is it? Well don't waste a scrap.

– What she talking at?
– Mum?
– He's got visitors is too right that's for sure ha!
– Say what Mum?
– A rat army come to feed on your old man's dead heart. Ha!
– Hell is alive, shadow of the tree, moonlight and demons, rats is inside him.
– Eating his soul. How's that for karma eh girls? Ha!
– Eating the insides of him.
– Cleaning up his bones, his dead useless bones.
– They're eating him.
– So you reap what you sow.
– But they're eating him.
– This is how it is girl, just what he knows.
– But they is inside him.
– You hold your nerve girl.
– But they're eating him, they're eating him!
– I say hush girl hush. Hear them crows? Come to carry away his soul.
– But they're inside him, they're in there eating him.
– He had the curse inside him long before these rats.
– It's not right. This is hell we brung.
– Like the beatings is right?
– Or the showings is right?
– But this don't make it so.
– And so what do you propose?
– They's gonna find out.
– If you keep up this nonsense they just bloody might.
– Let's just bury him.

– I'll seriously whack you if you don't shut up.

– As bad as him that make you as bad as him.

– Look around girl. Crows lined up watching on in the morning sun. It's too late.

– Morning Mum. Sorry 'bout me sister. She's just freaking out.

– Well you can hardly blame her, there are rats eating his insides out.

– Say morning Mum.

– Them crows is all watching.

– Say morning Mum, or I'll hit ya.

– Morning Mum.

– Morning sun, dream of my heart. It's a shocking thing to see I'll give you that.

– If we just say it was an accident.

– We don't have to say a thing girl. He never come home from the pub.

– If we go to them and just say we're real sorry and it was an accident.

– I'm going to ignore that.

– Like he just fell over or something.

– Now girls nothing has changed. Your dad and me what?

– They had a fight he's gone to his sister's.

– His sister's where this sister?

– I see his deadness you can't make up a story.

– Gone to his sister's? Sister where?

– Not gone anywhere but up in that tree on the block and tackle.

– Heave ho how'd you get him up there?

– The girls help ya did they?

– The three of you in cahoots is it, killed the man dead?

– I don't like to do this but you gone killed him dead.

– We is all real sorry.

– We is all real sorry and we wish we didn't have to.

– But we got to.

– We got to.

– We got to take you in for the murder of your nothing man.
– But if we just say.
– That slab of meat hanging there got more life in it now than when it was breathing. You better think about how cold that cell is sister. That raging nothing against those still walls. Now get on with your chores.
– The crows they is all staring at him.
– I wish we didn't. But we had to. So shut your head down and come do the chores.

VI

– No sooner you blink than fresh as a twig, out rings the trill of Mrs Smith.
– Holding a something appearing like magic at the kitchen gate.
– Too late to do anything as she barrels up and through.
– Hello love, bought you a cake.
– Heard you was missing your bloke.
– Causing a ruckus so everyone says.
– And now gone to his sister's they say?
– Looks hard, close, shit.
– You sure he not actually dead?
– Sweats and chills she's asking it straight.
– What do you do now, when the words they is said?
– Good bloody riddance love I bought you a present instead.
– Unwrapping the pie smiles with her face.
– That man was a dog. A slack-arse disgrace.
– We all know what he done, all that he is, we got your back love, that's just how it is.
– Word on the street is youse both had a fight, and old Mister Jones tells us he's left with the night. Got his coat and his hat left 'em in his truck. Gonna chuck them out soon with any luck.
– Good riddance, last of him I say.

- Gone forever let's hope love.
- Her eyes more lovely than the sun, grips me arm, what's done is done.
- Earth got a funny way of claiming back its stuff-ups lass.
- You know, my old man says something you might like to know. That even if he died you'd never know, easy to forget a mongrel like that. And if anyone comes asking well none of us'd know.
- I mean, he gone to his sister's right? That's what he done, oh I know her name, tip of me tongue. Said to me just the other day. Saw him down the shops and I ask him how he is. Says all fine he's off to his sis.
- Now what's her name, I swear he said it.
- Marjory?
- Marjory that it?
- Marjory yeah, another awful shit.
- Yes clear as the day it was, down at the thing, said I'm off to see me sister. Marjory.
- His sister Marjory.
- Says she lives somewhere, couldn't say. Not important, but I know what he said.
- And anyway, that's what we all say.
- The pie. Is lovely.
- All us ladies chipped in, an apple each. The men bought a log from each place that's his. Made a big fire love, an oven just for you. Make no mistake girls, that pastry baked with the heat from a dozen trees cut by another twenty more.
- Plenty of wood round here to fight a fire. Made with love, for you and your two girls.
- Steel eyes bore down to where the guilt shines and curls.
- Gulp it down girl. Gulp it down good. This story is told now, is you understood?
- Answer her.
- Yeah I's understood.
- And just like that with a smile and a flourish, she pulls out from her

pocket an envelope creased but with nothing written on it.

– And here, help you back on your feet, just a whip around. Now he's upped and left bit more of a help you might need.

– Grin's big and broad, wraps a full bosom shawl and leaves.

– Oo-roo love, godspeed!

– Open the paper pressed into your hand, inside some notes, hard-earned cash scraped together from the hard-made bits that they had.

– Oh my.

– Oh dear.

– Oh they has done a collection.

– A bloody big cheer.

– Sent out the hat.

– To cast off the rat.

– And the proceeds are clear.

– Congratulations for getting rid of that.

VII

– The moment girls, the moment is here.

– Into the yard where the chickens feed.

– On maggots dripping from his fleshy feast.

– Not a him no more is it. Just a bit of meat hanging there.

– Hasn't even got no eyes no more.

– A cloud of angry flies around the hole in his neck reaching into his face.

– Gag on that, a thousand chomping jaws.

– Death glow black a hungry snow, shapes that wriggle and spill and grow.

– Look at the girls, they is eating all the bugs and bits.

– Wrigglers like leaves, flesh hangs off in strips, overhead the call of crows.

Shari Sebbens in Griffin Theatre Company's 2015 production. (Photo: Brett Boardman)

– Some dance they sure is making.

– Never seen so much life in the yard.

– Look at that one trying to get a piece of him.

– Gets her beak onto it and rips off a bit of dangling skin.

– The stink don't seem to bother them none.

– Girls stand clear, shoo 'em back.

– Shoo shoo.

– Back you lot back!

– Bloody hell they're not listening, maybe they like this spot?

– Maggots is better than seeds I think.

– Girls, stand back. Untying him now.

– Stand back.

– Go on Mum let him have it.

– Swings still for a second in the hot air, then unfurls with a thud.

– His half-rotten full-cursed body stillborn in the dirt.

– Fists and wrists with bones poking through.

– Knuckles won't flay you now.

– Lookit them chooks wary, scoping him out.

– Bit unsure.

– They'll do their thing.

– In she plucks for a curious peck, and surprised delight as in sinks her beak.

– Cock cruises up, pushes her aside.

– Needed her to try it first though didn't he.

– And carcass tested, in they all come now furious and keen.

– Amidst the feathers and squawks flying, flesh-pecked holes are widening.

– Features fading as the whites of his bones appear.

– Look at them go.

- The father lord our master.
- His pecked-at cadaver.
- Blessed be thy name.
- You dead useless lump, dead as dead hereafter.
- Dead.
- Mr Dead.
- Goodbye Daddy dead now.
- Mr dead Daddy dead dead.
- Disappearing before our very eyes.

- His dick they're eating at his dick.
- No standing on ceremony ladies.
- There's something in this girls.
- I know what you mean Mum.
- I think I feel it too.
- What's it like to you girls?
- I don't know but it's kinda lifting. Like them clouds maybe … Like there's some plague or something, like then they clear, and it's like them skies is opening or something.
- Is what I feel too.
- Where he's going is inside their bellies.
- Making hungry girls happy.
- There's a curse on them dead-picked bones girls. The makings of him inside them, come out the other end and feed the dirt, flowers grow in this shit come from his blood.
- You love them roses right Mum?
- Used to love a rose and we used to wonder why they all die.
- The sight of him. Stamping on 'em. Pissing on 'em. Pouring his juice on 'em. Talking at them. Like they was his to control.

– Mum?

– Yes.

– Mum you look sad.

– Do I?

– You know a man that has to take his rage out on a flower tree ain't much of a man you know that right?

– Mum?

– I'm going to boil his bones.

– Boil his bones?

– Boil up the copper. Gonna make a stock from his bones.

– Mum?

– I'm gonna make me a rose garden, the best he never seen. One you can marvel at, sit and ponder his departure. That dead hole in his head can stare back at me in every blossom, stare back at the place what he's left, that one what brings life to the soil, that brings life to this soil, that brings life to this soil …

– Mum?

– Girls what did I say? Boil up the copper.

– She gone cold and white, folding eyes small.

– Mum?

– Mum?

– I said this hole in his head is more beautiful than alive, we gonna boil up his bones, those wretched bones, make a tonic for the yard.

– Make flowers grow.

– Where this cruelty go now but back into the soil.

– Watch her, what we do?

– I don't know.

– Mum?

– Mum please.

– Mum I said, shit.

– Shake her.

– Mum.

- You gotta come back.
- Please Mum.
- Shake her. Hit her.
- Mum!
- I said whack.
- Mum please don't go, so close now you stay!
- Hit her just once to see what she say.
- Mum!
- Bloody hell she's gone off with the pixies.
- Mum!
- Mum!
- Slap her.
- Hit her.
- Break out of it Mum.
- We need you Mum.
- Glazed eyes.
- Mum?
- You gotta get with it Mum.
- Black raven-circling eyes. We killed him dead. Eating his eyes.
- Yeah we did what we had to. You said.
- Stop your crazy head.
- Silent the earth. Doesn't want it either I suppose.
- Oh crap. Mum.
- Hit her again.
- Whack!

- Then hey, stop that.
- Hey you stop that!
- A bloody call.
- Bloody hell a bloody voice makes a call.
- Shit who's that?

– Man's voice makes a call.

– What's going on here?

– Hear the man's call.

– Stop that!

– Spin, the three of us, there coming across the yard is Postie Steve.

– Half copper half postie Steve.

– Shit.

– Half copper half postie Steve.

– Steve.

– Post office man.

– Police office man.

– Shit.

– Steve the postie copper Steve, thing what passes for judge and detective round here.

– Nothing worse could happen right now.

– You three, what's this, hitting at your mum?!

– He's coming across towards us, quick, run.

– Don't run dickhead.

– Head him off go that way.

– You grab a stick and I'll whack him away.

– Girls.

– Mum we gotta pray.

– Girls I said stop.

– Mum.

– Stevens. Hello.

– He's coming up quick.

– You okay Missus, girls pulling a trick?

– No we were playing our games.

– That's strange.

– Walk towards him, follow suit, get the woodpile between him and us and the chooks.

– Don't look back.
– Steer him away.
– Just games you say?
– He's got whiskers all over his face and his neck.
– Dark eyes like slits.
– Hands like plates.
– Hat old and sweat-stained.
– Old grumpy prick.
– Is everything okay here? I haven't seen your old man. There's a parcel at the station for him.
– Parcel?
– Yeah parcel, it's in the truck.
– Must be something thinks will change his luck.
– He not around, word is he left town?
– Stare.
– Gulp.
– Been off to see his sister.
– Sister? Didn't know he had a sister.
– Yeah, lives up north, hot up there.
– Oh right. Yeah he caused a bloody stink the other night. Bluing on he was making a ruckus, surprised he got home alright. Angry he got the place that's for sure.
– Doesn't sound like him.
– Both share a grin.
– Yeah wouldn't have surprised me if he turned up dead.
– Quiet.
– Sorry Missus, awfully uncouth.
– Marjory her name is, up north.
– His sister the bastard.
– Bastard Marjory the Bitch.
– Girls.

– Don't like your aunty girls?
– Smiles he does.
– Real prick she is. Mum and her hated each other's guts.
– Okay girls.
– Grinning Stevens is what he is.
– Maybe he's alright this Stevens.
– Yeah well his parcel, it's in the truck. I'll go grab it for luck.
– Stops.
– Halts.
– Sees.
– Catches his head as it twitches.
– Holy fuck.
– He sees.
– Shit he sees.
– The clucking of the chooks is coming now thick.
– The call of the crows and the hell through the trees.
– He sees, oh shit he sees.
– Looking past the woodpile, to the girls manic feast.
– The sky with them black birds roving in circling ease.
– What the blazes is all that going on over there?
– And moving now he is, moving towards them.
– Hurrying up towards them.
– Oh shit.
– Shit.
– Shit stop him.
– How?
– Bloody I don't know.
– And he stops.
– Stops.
– Turns his head and gulps.
– Looks down the ground.

– Away with a frown.
– Looks back around eyes wide and hollow.
– Gulping back a sick.
– Fuck.
– Gone to his sister's he says?
– Looks up.
– Gone to his grave more bloody likely.
– Oh shit.
– Staring cold.
– Oh fucking shit.
– How?
– Nothing comes.
– How he this?
– Nothing from the three of us.
– They're eating him. They're eating him?
– Horror on him now.
– He's got a look in him now.
– Wild in him now.
– Eating him. They're eating him. The chickens is eating him.
– Gulps back more sick.
– Can't believe it.
– Can't believe it.
– Won't look at it.
– They're eating him. Jesus.
– Step up she does, Mum charged with power.
– Steps up like a snorting beast to tower.
– Yeah they're eating him. Eating his rotten corpse. Been hanging by the tree there in the hot sun, gettin' the stink on, flies come making, maggots been breeding, the girls get a feeding, worth more dead than alive is what he is. You know it like we do.
– Mum's gone cold staring back at him.

– He gulps doesn't know where to look.

– You wanna say something Stevens is it? You want to say something now is it you? All the times you see you knew. His hands like fucking hammers, his fists like molten rain, his fucking mouth and his violence always been the same. But what do you do Stevens? What do you and all them menfolk do? Ya let him. Ya let him do what he do. Ya let him do what he do cos it's not your business is it Stevens. None of yours is it man. Don't stick your bloody nose into anybody else's business that the authorised plan?

– But they're eating him.

– Yeah?

– It's not right.

– Well call the bloody police then Sergeant. Call them and tell them that so. You got old Missus Bloody Wallop here feeding her chickens the fucking so and so. Go on then.

– Stumbles over to a stump. Bends his knees, collapses down.

– Lets out a breath all slow.

– Fuck.

– You can say that again.

– How'd he die?

– I shot him in the neck.

– Shot him in the neck?

– I knocked his knees out.

– I conked him on the head.

– The three of us Mister, we killed him dead.

– Looks up and around.

– Nobody been to ask where he been instead, I mean work?

– Work?

– Ha!

– Nobody ask yet?

– None asks, no tell.

– Nobody wishes to know what we might tell.

– Some men it just isn't worth the speaking of.

– Some men less said the better.

– Nobody been around to ask?

– Nobody. Quiet out here.

– Raises an eyebrow.

– Quiet out here yeah that's for sure.

– Glint like evil in his eyes.

– Killed him you said?

– I killed him, shot him in the neck.

– I knocked his knees out.

– I banged him on the head.

– The three of youse did him? And nobody been around to ask?

– Not a one. Just you.

– Grabs both his knees pulls himself up. Hands on hips, gives a low whip.

– What's he whistle for?

– No sooner you ask it, but an old blue comes bounding round the house, comes to him. The chickens scatter like confetti.

– Old Blue stands by his side.

– Bloke says something silent dog listens to, then trots to sniff the bloke through.

– Dog sniffs it. Smells the dead on the thing.

– Looks back at his master.

– Comes straight back to sit.

– Eyes gazing upwards, mouth hard and set.

– Tail low, ears erect.

– Postie Steve rubs the dog's neck, kisses his nuzzle, walks him over.

Now get.

- Quizzical look, instantly set.
- And with a pounce he's on the thing, and he's in there making like it's Sunday lunch. He's gone for what's left of the balls, and the thighs. He's tearing into the ribs and exposing the insides. A rat comes flying out and he pays it no heed. He gets hold of that maggoty heart and he's chowing on in like a fiend.
- The bloody dog's gone apeshit with greed.
- And the thing runs round and he lifts up his head and he barks low and long and back the other side and gets to those knees.
- Snarling teeth bared he rips them apart. Chews through twisted fabrics. Sinews and leathery parts.
- The dog's got a routine, he's going hard.
- Old man, your old man, was known round these parts.
- Stevie Postie Copper speaks.
- He makes a sound or two, points to a space left. The dog goes onto the hips and gets his teeth round the pelvis. With a crack his grip breaks through.
- Another gesture, and Blue's on his ribs, cracks another one through.
- The head, skull, start with the nose Blue.
- Postie Steve is telling him what to do.
- Crack. The bloody thing's not doing it by halves old Blue.
- Stevens once had a dog, her name was Blue, she had a full litter, and her first love was true. That's me, Stevens. This dog here is Blue.
- She looks up. Then gets back to it.
- Oh it was true she had the thing for those little ones. Gone lost them one night, when a drunk passing by saw to that. Yeah, a drunk what looked strangely like a man you girls once knew.
- What's he saying?
- You saying?
- Dog never forgets a face.
- Cold he is now.

– Kicked 'em to death this bloke youse once knew. Kicked 'em to death in front of her. Had her chained up. Couldn't stop him but she howled for months.

– He kicked the pups to death?

– Stamped on their heads.

– Oh sweet Lord Jesus and Christ in heaven not what you said.

– You might not want to hear that ladies, but that's how it was. And she never forgets this one. Come here Blue.

– Dropping all its work, dog trots over, comes to him, pats her on the head.

– Water.

– She laps at the tap.

– Yeah, well you've gone gotten yourselves the hard ones broken up.

– Hard ones, say what he mean?

– The bones I mean.

– The skull and the sternum and the pelvis, bloody hell.

– They're always a bugger to break. Need a hammer or some such. Or a vengeful dog, they say every old blue gets her day. Rubs her on the head.

– Sighs, pats her close and sweet.

– Laps out her tongue for a treat.

– Cricks his neck. Hands on his hips.

– Best be off.

– Starts on his walk.

– Turns, halts.

– Yeah right so I got his parcel so when he gets back from his sister's tell him it's at the office. It's obvious there's no sign of him here.

– Tips his hat and goes.

– Saunters off and goes.

– Just tips his hat and takes his dog and he's off.

– Like that.

– Like that.
– Bloody Stevens The Postie Copper been come and gone like that.

VIII

– Steam rises off the pot, them flames is licking, the night is loud is so silent.
– The latch on the run left off on purpose.
– At some point tonight, tonight they will come.
– The smell of blood they been tasting, three nights now they come.
– Them foxy foxes, bursting in to steal lives.
– Them chickens what ate our dad.
– The bastard.
– Showing's no more.
– Foxy-feast treats on the floor.
– On chickens' meat.
– On his misery heart.
– Gone to his sister's aye.
– Up north somewhere, couldn't tell you.
– Couldn't say.
– Grinder, on the bench.
– Mixed with more water.
– Clothes go in too.
– The liquid, grainy, lumpy, boil it some more.
– Bring more roses ladies, come on help the cook!
– You grow a new garden Ma?
– I grow one for you.
– What colours you after?
– Any'll do.
– Any?
– Yeah, any but his.

– The colour of his gaping hole where all hell pokes through.

– Just three days it takes, to be rid of his spell.

– Patience and good luck, some the universe sends.

–   The dead hole where his place was, makes its own amends.

MUM *serves up three bowls of soup.*

They sup together.

END

www.ingramcontent.com/pod-product-compliance
Lightning Source LLC
Chambersburg PA
CBHW050025090426
42734CB00021B/3431